The Box in the Loft

By Cameron Macintosh

"It is my big day!" said Stan.
"I am six!"

Stan was happy with
his gifts.

"But I wish Nan was here,"
said Stan.

He was a bit sad.

"There is one gift left,"
said Dad.
"It's up in the loft."

"I do not like that loft,"
said Stan.

"But the gift is in a big box!"
said Dad.

"Let's go up."

Up in the loft, Dad slid
the big box to Stan.

"Lift off the lid," said Dad.

"Nan left this box for you,"
Dad said.

In the box were a soft fox
and lots of photos.

"Look at this, Stan,"
said Dad.

For Stan,
when he is six.
Lots of love,
from Nan.

"I am glad I came up, Dad,"
said Stan.
"This is the best gift."

For Stan,
when he is six.
Lots of love,
from Nan.

CHECKING FOR MEANING

1. How old is Stan on his birthday? *(Literal)*

2. What was in the box in the loft? *(Literal)*

3. Why isn't Nan with Stan on his birthday? *(Inferential)*

EXTENDING VOCABULARY

gift	What is a *gift*? What is another word that has a similar meaning? E.g. present.
left	What does *left* mean in this story? What other meanings does it have? Can you use it in different sentences to show its meanings?
best	What does it mean if something is the *best*? Explain that the words we use to describe the quality of something are *good*, *better* and *best*.

MOVING BEYOND THE TEXT

1. Why do you think Nan left photos in the box for Stan?

2. Why is a loft a good place to keep things? Where do you keep things at home that you don't use very often?

3. What is the best gift you have ever received? Why was it the best?

4. If you bought a gift for a good friend, what would you buy? Why?

SPEED SOUNDS

ft	mp	nd	nk	st

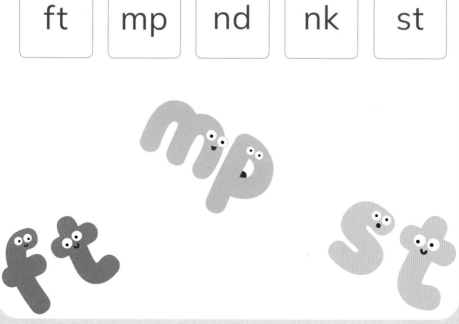

PRACTICE WORDS

left

gift

loft

gifts

Lift

soft

and

best